ISBN 0 531 17151 5

Library of Congress Catalog
Card Number: 88-83090

Design	David West
	Children's Book Design
Editor	Margaret Fagan
Researcher	Cecilia Weston-Baker
Illustrators	Aziz Khan
	Galina Zolfaghari
Consultants	Alan Morton, PhD
	Science Museum, London
	John Warren, PhD
	Formerly Reader in Physics Education
	Brunel University, London

© Aladdin Books Ltd
Designed and produced by
Aladdin Books Ltd
70 Old Compton Street
London W1

First Published in the
United States in 1989 by
Gloucester Press
387 Park Avenue South
New York, NY 10016

Printed in Belgium

HANDS · ON · SCIENCE

RAINBOWS TO LASERS

Kathryn Whyman

GLOUCESTER PRESS
New York · London · Toronto · Sydney

CONTENTS

This book introduces the subject of light — from rainbows in the natural world to the technology of lasers. Every page begins with new ideas set out in an easy-to-follow way which is shown below. There are "hands-on" projects for you to do and quizzes to enjoy. They will help you to learn more about light.

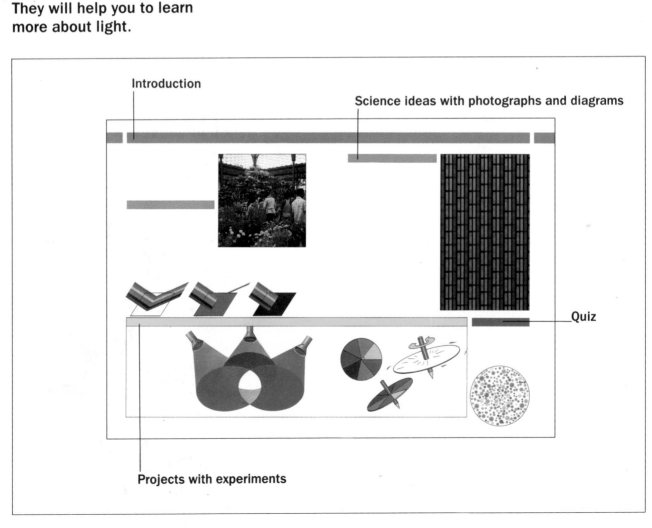

Introduction

Science ideas with photographs and diagrams

Quiz

Projects with experiments

Introduction

Without sunlight there would be no life on Earth. Green plants use carbon dioxide, water and sunlight to make new substances in a process called photosynthesis. Then animals eat the plants and use the chemicals they get from the plants to grow. Indirectly, we depend on sunlight for our survival and food.

Light makes the world bright and colorful. You see the things around you when light is reflected into your eyes. You can see sizes, shapes, and colors. You may also use special instruments to help you see very small or very distant things — such as the cells which make up your body, or the stars in the sky. This book will help you find out about light and the way you see. You can see how light behaves in different circumstances — from rainbows to lasers.

Lasers are used to produce dramatic effects

Sunlight appears colorless but really it is made up of different colors. Sometimes you can see these colors — on the surfaces of bubbles or if there is oil on water. You may also see the colors across the sky in the form of a rainbow. In each case "white" light is being separated into different colors called the spectrum.

HOW A RAINBOW IS MADE

When the Sun comes out during a shower you may see a rainbow. The sunlight shines on the droplets of rain and gets separated into the colors of the spectrum. From a distance the light appears as a colored arc across the sky. People divide the rainbow into seven bands of color — red, orange, yellow, green, blue, indigo and violet. The colors always appear in the same order, with red on the outside and violet on the inside of the arc. The diagram shows how light which enters each raindrop is reflected, bent and separated into all the colors of the spectrum, which together form a rainbow in the sky.

△ It is impossible to reach the end of a rainbow — you can only see it shining in the sky at a distance.

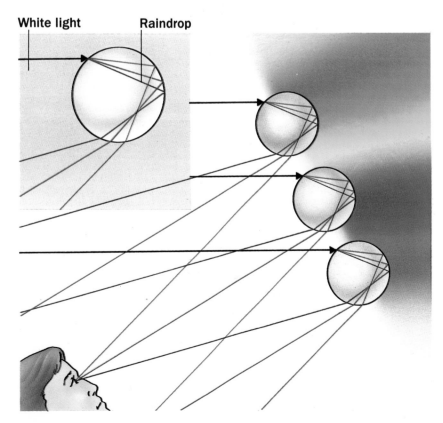

White light   Raindrop

MAKE A RAINBOW

You can see the colors of the spectrum by making your own rainbow. On a sunny day fill a pan of water and rest a mirror at an angle inside it. Stand the pan in front of a window so that sunlight falls onto the mirror. Then hold a piece of white cardboard in front of the mirror and move it around until you see a rainbow appear on it. You may have to move the mirror to get this right. The mirror and the water act as a "prism" — they separate white light into the colors of the spectrum.

THE NORTHERN LIGHTS

Sometimes dazzling displays of colored lights appear in the sky at night in parts of the world which are far from the equator. These lights are caused by huge explosions on the surface of the Sun known as "flares." During a flare, millions of tiny particles are sent out from the Sun. They travel very fast and some eventually reach the Earth's atmosphere. The Earth's magnetism bends the paths of the particles so they only reach the Earth's atmosphere near the poles. As they travel through the air they bump into other particles. These collisions produce light. In the North they can be seen best in parts of Canada, but they can also be seen in northern Scotland and Scandinavia. They are called the Northern Lights or "Aurora borealis." Similar lights can be seen in the South where they are called "Aurora australis."

△ The Northern Lights make an impressive display of color which looks like a constantly moving curtain in the sky.

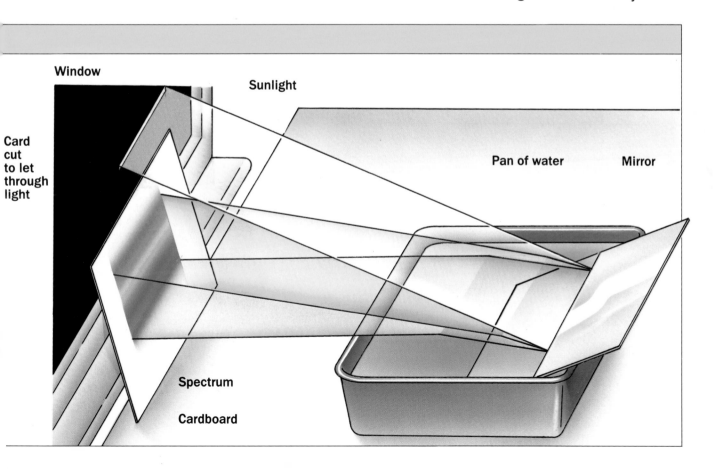

Window

Sunlight

Card cut to let through light

Pan of water

Mirror

Spectrum

Cardboard

Light always travels in straight lines called rays. Some substances allow light to travel through them. These are called transparent substances. But opaque substances do not let light through them. When light falls onto an opaque substance like metal or wood, a shadow may be cast behind the object.

ECLIPSES

The Earth and the Moon are constantly traveling around the Sun. Sometimes the Moon passes between the Sun and the Earth. When this happens the Moon blocks light because it is opaque and a shadow is cast on the Earth. If you are on the part of the Earth in total shadow, the Sun will appear to be completely hidden by the Moon. This is called a "total eclipse of the Sun." Other parts of the Earth will be in partial shadow. From these areas only part of the Sun will be hidden by the Moon. This is called a partial eclipse of the Sun.

△ In a total eclipse of the Sun only the Sun's outer atmosphere shines around the Moon.

▽ Shadows are strongest in bright light. These trees cast several shadows as they block light from the Sun.

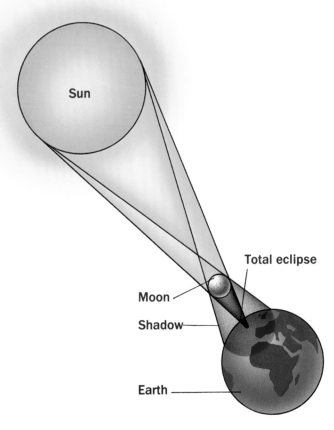

Sun

Total eclipse

Moon

Shadow

Earth

WITHOUT SHADOWS

To take a good photograph it is important to have just the right lighting. The person being photographed (the subject) needs to be well lit by floodlights. But this light could cast a shadow on the screen behind. To get rid of this shadow the photographer uses "backlights" placed on each side of, and slightly behind, the subject. The backlights light the screen to get rid of the shadows. This lighting should produce a perfect photograph without unwanted shadows.

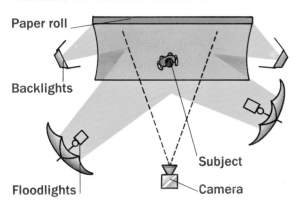

Paper roll

Backlights

Floodlights

Subject

Camera

△ The lights being used to take this photograph provide just the right illumination with no shadows to spoil the results.

MAKE A SHADOW CLOCK

During the day the Sun appears to move across the sky. It casts different shadows at different times. You can use the Sun to tell the time with this shadow clock. Place the clock on a sheet of white paper so it faces the Sun. Mark where the shadow falls and write the time beside the mark. Do this several times until your clock is complete.

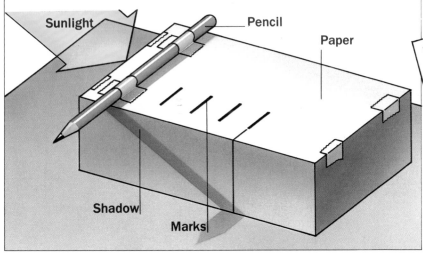

Sunlight

Pencil

Paper

Shadow

Marks

QUIZ

These pictures show the same person in the same place on the same day. Can you explain why the shadows are different lengths and point in different directions?

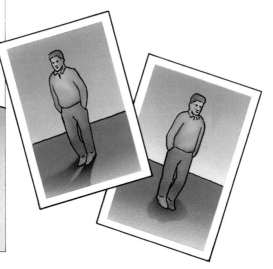

When light from the Sun or from an electric light bulb reaches an object some of it bounces off again. This is called reflection. It is this reflected light that you see when you look at something. Mirrors are good reflectors so are surfaces like this white sheet of paper.

REFLECTION

The diagram shows how you might see a reflection of a friend in water. Sunlight falls on the friend. Some of this light is reflected straight into your eyes. This allows you to see your friend. But some of the light is reflected onto the water between you. Because water reflects some of the light, some of it bounces back up to your eyes. Light normally travels in straight lines so it seems to you that this reflection is coming from below the water. Flat, shiny surfaces like glass, water and polished metals reflect light very well. You may see a reflection of yourself when you look into them.

△ On a sunny day in calm water a reflection can look almost as real as the scene itself — but it is really just an illusion.

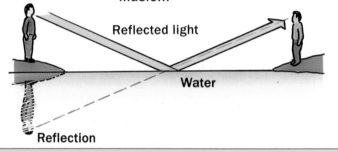

Reflected light

Water

Reflection

MAKE YOUR OWN PERISCOPE

Periscopes can help you see over walls and around corners. You can make one yourself by following the instructions in the diagrams. Start by cutting the cardboard so that the mirrors are a little wider than the periscope case. Make sure you cut the holes and slots to fit the mirrors too. Carefully slot the mirrors in position as shown. Do you know how the reflecting mirrors allow you to see around corners?

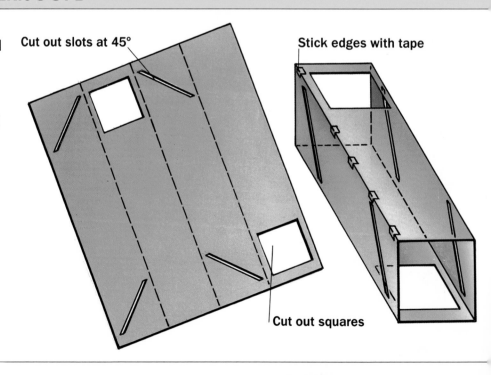

Cut out slots at 45°

Stick edges with tape

Cut out squares

CONVEX AND CONCAVE

Not all mirrors are flat — some kinds are curved. A mirror that curves inward is called a concave mirror. A mirror that curves outward is known as a convex mirror. The reflections from curved mirrors look different to those from flat mirrors. You can see this by looking at yourself in a spoon. The front of the spoon is like a concave mirror and in it you will appear upside down. But if you bring the spoon very close to you, you will see a large image of your eye the right way up. The back of the spoon is like a convex mirror — in it your reflection will be upright but small.

CONVEX

Sight

Image is upright and smaller, the further away you are

CONCAVE

Sight

Image is upside-down unless very close

Spoon

△ Have you ever been in "the hall of mirrors" at an amusement park? These mirrors make people look very strange — like the people in the photograph. They use mirrors which curve in and out. Some parts of the mirrors are convex and some are concave. Your reflection is stretched in some places and squeezed together in others.

QUIZ

Even flat mirrors can be misleading. Can you read the sentence below? It has been written in mirror writing. Try reading it in a mirror — you will find it much easier.

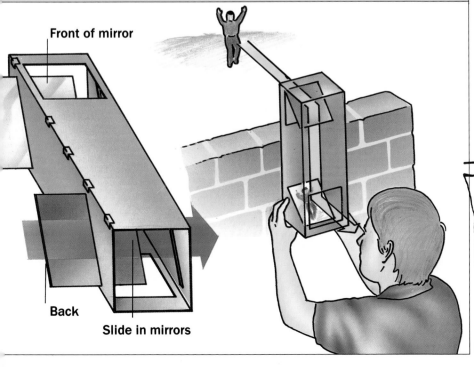

Front of mirror

Back

Slide in mirrors

How well can you read backwards without using a Mirror?

Although light travels in straight lines you have seen how it can be reflected and made to change direction. Light travels at different speeds through different substances. When light passes from one substance to another, it may also change direction. This process, refraction, makes light appear to bend.

REAPPEARING COIN

You can see the effects of how light appears to bend for yourself. Try this experiment using a bowl, a coin, and some water. Put the coin in the bottom of the bowl and move backward until the coin just disappears from sight. Stand still while a friend pours water into the bowl. You should find that the coin comes into view again. This happens because the water causes the light from the coin to change direction so that it travels to your eyes.

△ The straw in the photograph appear to be bent. Light from the straw is being refracted as it passes from the water to the air.

Line of sight will not reveal coin

▷ Reflectors are able to collect light from one direction and reflect it back in the same direction.

MIRAGE

People in the desert sometimes think they see water. But this is really just an illusion known as a mirage. You may have seen mirages yourself on the road on a hot day. Mirages are caused by refraction of light as it passes through air of different temperatures. On a hot day the air near the ground is much hotter than air higher up. As the light passes from the cooler air to the hotter air it gets refracted and appears to come from a point nearer the viewer. This makes objects appear closer than they are.

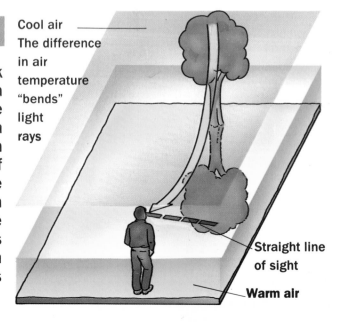

Cool air

The difference in air temperature "bends" light rays

Straight line of sight

Warm air

FIBER OPTICS

Optical fibers are used to channel light from place to place. They are solid glass rods which are as thin as hair. They are flexible and can be bent and twisted like wire. Light travels along the fiber by bouncing from side to side along the length of the rod. There is a cladding which surrounds bundles of the rods to protect them from damage and to prevent light coming into the cable.

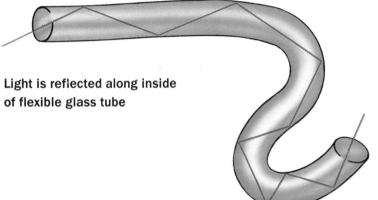

Light is reflected along inside of flexible glass tube

△ Optical fibers are already being used by telephone companies. They can carry more information than electric cables and are likely to be used more in the future. The optical fibers carry information as light signals. These signals travel at the speed of light in the material.

REFLECTORS

If you have a bicycle it will probably have "reflectors" fitted to it. These help other road users to see your bicycle at night. Underneath the smooth outer surface of a reflector there is a layer of plastic shaped with many angles. The angles ensure that any light falling on the reflector is reflected back to source. Reflectors worn by the police work in the same way to ensure motorists can see them.

Light is reflected
back to source

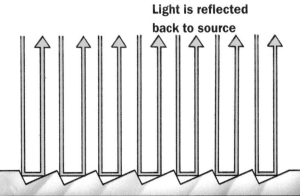

Lenses are specially shaped pieces of transparent material like glass or plastic. They are curved on one or both sides, and can be used to refract ("bend") light. They may make objects appear larger or smaller. They are used in instruments which help us to see things we cannot see with our eyes alone.

TYPES OF LENSES

Lenses that curve outward are called convex lenses. Lenses that curve inward are called concave lenses. The diagram below shows what happens to light as it passes through each type of lens. Light passing through the convex lens is bent inward — it converges. Light passing through the concave lens is bent outward — it diverges. Convex lenses can magnify small objects, but things appear smaller when they are seen through a concave lens.

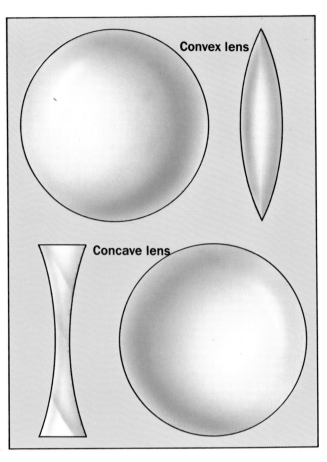

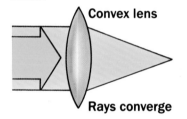

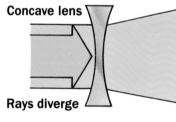

△ The drawing shows lenses as they appear from the front and the side. Convex lenses are thicker in the middle than at the edges. But concave lenses are thicker at the edges.

THE LIGHT MICROSCOPE

A microscope is an instrument that is used to make small objects — especially tiny living things or cells — appear larger so they can be studied. A very thin slice of the specimen to be viewed is placed on a glass slide and lit up by a light attached below. The light passes through the specimen on the glass slide and then through a number of lenses. The lenses magnify the image of the object by refracting the light so that it diverges. Microscopes can magnify things so that they appear hundreds of times larger than their real size. They are often used by doctors and scientists working in laboratories.

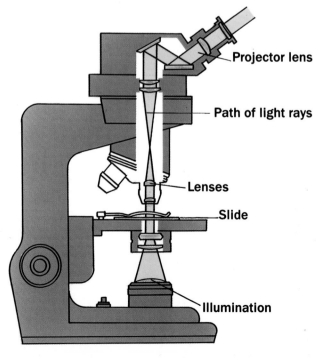

TELESCOPES

Astronomers use telescopes to study the night sky. Telescopes allow distant objects — such as planets or groups of stars — to be seen more clearly. Telescopes gather light so they make images clearer. There are two main types of telescope. The top diagram shows a refracting telescope. This uses a lens to collect and focus light from the sky and a smaller lens to magnify the image. The reflecting telescope below uses two mirrors to reflect light through a small lens. This lens then magnifies the image.

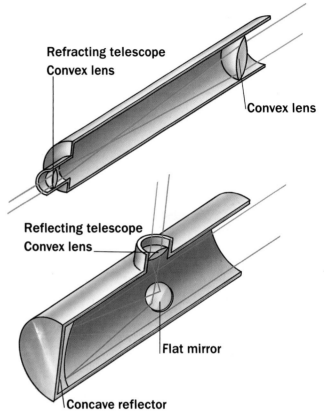

Refracting telescope
Convex lens

Convex lens

Reflecting telescope
Convex lens

Flat mirror

Concave reflector

◁ This telescope is designed for observing the night sky. A system of lenses collects light so that the stars can be more clearly seen.

MAKE YOUR OWN TELESCOPE

Stand a shaving mirror by a window so that it points towards the Moon. Then hold a flat mirror so that you can see a reflection of the shaving mirror in it. Look at the reflection in the flat mirror through a magnifying glass, — the Moon will look brighter. **WARNING: Always look at the night sky. Viewing the Sun through a telescope is dangerous.**

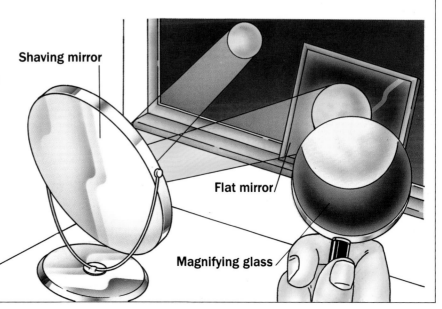

Shaving mirror

Flat mirror

Magnifying glass

You see things when light is reflected from them into your eyes. When there is no light, you cannot see. Your eyes enable you to see things in color and in focus. They also help you to judge distances. Your eyes receive images, and these are sent as impulses along nerves to your brain, which interprets them.

EYEBALLS

Your eyes are designed to receive reflected light, focus it, and send messages to your brain. Covering the front of your eye is a transparent protective coating called the cornea. Behind this is a circle of muscle called the iris. The iris has a hole in its center known as the pupil. Light enters the eye through the pupil and then passes through the lens. The lens is convex and focuses the light on a sort of screen at the back of the eye called the retina. You will see in the diagram that the image is upside down. Details of the image are sent along the optic nerve to the brain where the image is turned around.

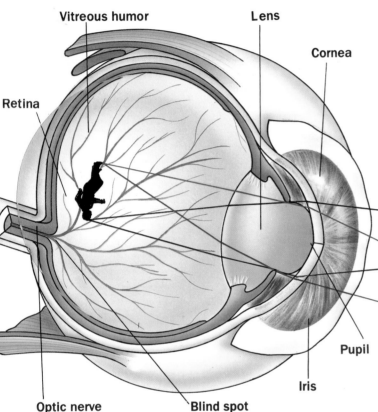

Vitreous humor · Lens · Cornea · Retina · Pupil · Iris · Optic nerve · Blind spot

FINDING OUT ABOUT SIGHT

You can do some simple experiments to find out more about your eyes. First of all, hold this page at arm's length in front of your right eye and stare at the magician. Now close your left eye and slowly move the page nearer to you. You will find that the frog disappears. This happens when the image of the frog falls on your blind spot - an area of the retina that does not pass signals to the brain. Judging distances is easier with two eyes than one. Draw a spot on a piece of cardboard about two feet in front of you. Try to touch the spot, first with both eyes and then with one closed. What do you notice?

Make the frog disappear

EYE PROBLEMS

You will only see clearly when the image of the object you are looking at falls exactly on your retina. If it falls in front of, or behind, the retina, the image will be blurred. Some people find it hard to see things which are close to them, but see distant objects clearly. They are "far sighted." Other people cannot see things which are far away. They are "near sighted." Sight can be improved by wearing glasses. Far sighted people wear glasses with convex lenses while near sighted people wear glasses with concave lenses. The diagrams below show how glasses change the direction of the light before it enters the eye so that the light falls exactly on the retina.

△ Many people wear glasses in order to correct their vision. Others choose to wear contact lenses as the tiny lenses hardly show.

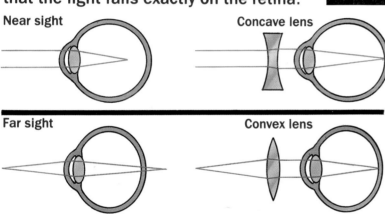

Near sight

Concave lens

Far sight

Convex lens

QUIZ

Sometimes the messages sent to your brain are confusing so your brain does not always interpret images correctly. The images shown here are called optical illusions. Try them out yourself and on your friends. 1. Are the lines straight or curved? 2. Which of these lines is longer? 3. Which figure is the tallest? Check your answers. Did you get them right or was your brain confused by the illusions?

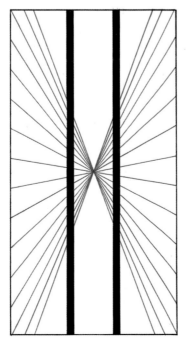

Most objects do not produce light of their own. Instead they *reflect* light which falls on them. The color an object appears depends on the color of light it reflects. There are only three primary colors of light — red, blue and green. All other colors are made by mixing these primary colors together.

REFLECTING COLOR

Ordinary white sunlight or electric light is made up of many colors. The diagrams below show how the colors reflected by an object give it its color. Something which appears white reflects all the colors in white light. However, an object which appears red reflects only red light — the other colors of the spectrum will be absorbed by the object. Something which appears black does not reflect any light at all — all the colors of the spectrum are completely absorbed.

△ You can see plants of many different colors in the photograph. Each one is reflecting a different combination of colored light into your eyes.

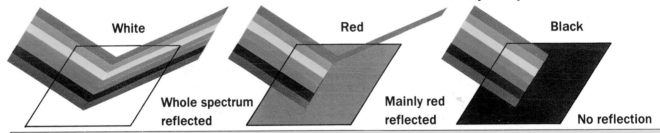

White — Whole spectrum reflected

Red — Mainly red reflected

Black — No reflection

MIXING COLORS WITH LIGHT

Different combinations of colored light mix to make different colors. You can try mixing light yourself. Put colored transparent paper — one red, one green and one blue — over the ends of three flashlights. Shine them onto white paper. Divide a circle into seven equal segments and color them with the colors of the spectrum. Spin the circle. What do you see?

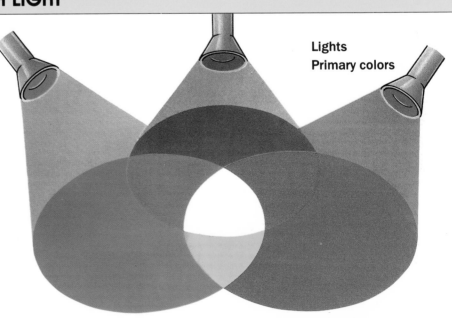

Lights
Primary colors

COLOR TELEVISION

A television receives signals from transmitters and turns them into pictures. The inside of the television screen is coated with many dots of special chemicals called phosphors. These dots are arranged in groups of three, so that each tiny part of the screen can produce all the three primary colors of light—red, blue and green. As the signal comes into the television it is translated into a pattern of colored dots on the screen. If you look closely at a television picture you will see that it is made up of lots of tiny colored dots. As the pattern of red, blue and green changes, so the picture and the colors it appears change too. To your eye the dots merge to form a single picture with many varieties of color and contrast.

▷ The picture shows part of a color television screen magnified. You can see that the picture is made up of lots of tiny red, blue and green dots. These dots combine to make all the colors you see on the screen.

Colors of the rainbow

Spin

Put pencil through circle

NEWTON'S WHEEL
When spinning all the colors appear white

Some people find it difficult to see colors. What number can you see in the dots below? If you cannot see a number you probably do not have normal color vision.

Answer: 4

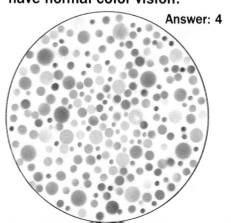

Different objects reflect different colors. This is because of a variety of substances they contain called pigments. Different pigments reflect different combinations of colors. Paints and dyes contain pigments. They can be used to change the color of things by changing the colors they reflect.

BLUE AND YELLOW MAKE GREEN

Many objects contain more than one pigment. You can mix paints to see how the pigments combine to give different colors. Mixing pigments is quite different from mixing lights. The primary colors of pigments are said to be red, blue and yellow — but more accurately they are magenta, cyan and yellow. All colors can be made by mixing these primary colors. Mixing blue with yellow makes green. This is because blue paint (cyan) reflects violet, blue and green light. Yellow pigment appears yellow because it reflects red, orange, yellow and green light. The only color which both pigments reflect is green. Mixing all three primary colors makes black, since between them the pigments absorb all colors of light.

Printed color photographs are made by combining dots of the primary colors on the page. Use a magnifying glass to look at the dots that make up the photograph on the opposite page. Apart from magenta, cyan, and yellow, black is used to give extra contrast.

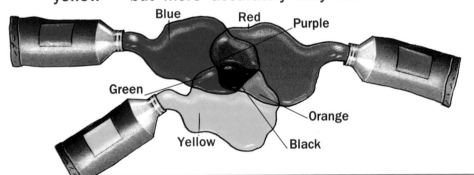

Blue   Red   Purple
Green
Orange
Yellow   Black

▷ These materials have been dyed bright colors to make them more attractive. Dyes can be made from plants or they may be man-made.

USING CHROMATOGRAPHY

You can separate the pigments used in colored pens and inks. This is called chromatography. Cut a strip of blotting paper and draw a line of ink about 2 inches from one end. Hang the strip so that the end nearest the ink just dips into a dish of water. The pigments will soon spread up the paper. Each pigment travels at a different speed and so they separate. When the color is at the top of the paper take it out and let it dry.

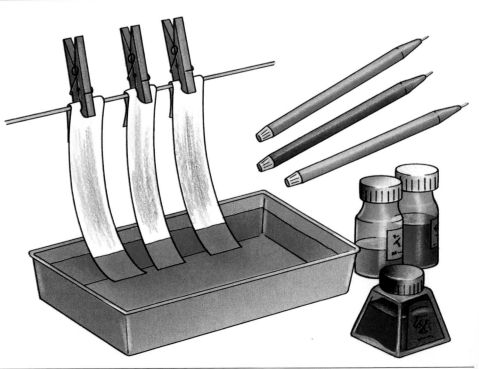

MAKING DYES

You can make vegetable dyes to color material. You can use cherries (red), onion skins (yellow) and spinach (green), as well as many others. Ask an adult to boil the leaves or fruit in a pan with a little water and simmer the mixture for 15 minutes. When it has cooled, put a coffee filter into a funnel and pour the liquid through it into a pan. Leave the material you want to dye in the pan for a few minutes and then let it dry.

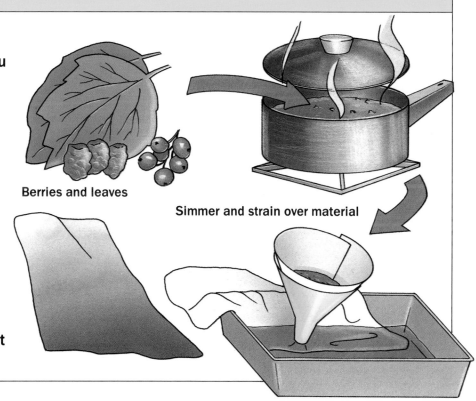

Berries and leaves

Simmer and strain over material

The Sun provides most of the light we need during the daytime but we need other sources of light after sunset. The simplest way to make light is with fire, for example in the form of a candle. But the most popular and convenient source of artificial light today is electric light.

HOW A LIGHT BULB WORKS

When a light is switched on, electricity flows through the filament, a thin coil of tungsten wire. Because the wire is so thin it gets very hot — as hot as 4,800°F. When electricity passes through it, the filament glows white and gives out light. There is no air in the bulb so that the filament does not burn out. It may be filled with another gas or with nothing at all — a " vacuum."

△ Electric light enables us to carry on with our lives even after the Sun has set. Once darkness falls, most cities are illuminated by millions of electric lights.

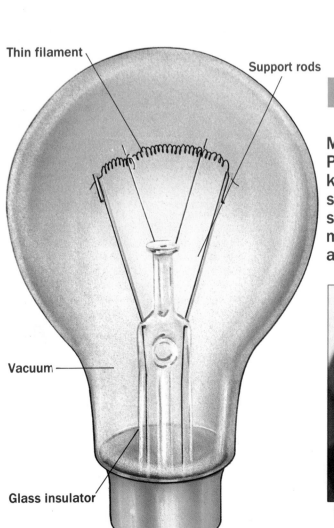

Thin filament

Support rods

Vacuum

Glass insulator

MEASURING LIGHT LEVELS

Many people need to measure light. Photographers and movie makers need to know how bright the light is in their studios. Light levels are important for some sports like baseball and tennis. To measure light levels accurately you need a light meter.

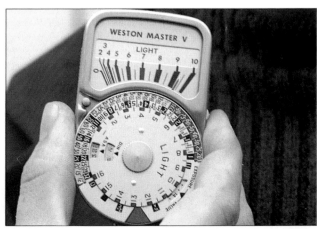

DIFFERENT ARTIFICIAL LIGHTS

Electric light bulbs may be convenient ways of lighting our homes but they are not suitable for all forms of lighting. Neon lights, used for street signs, and strip lights, used indoors, are both types of electric light. But they do not have a filament — instead they are filled with a gas which produces light when an electric current passes through it. To produce the figures on a digital watch or calculator a liquid crystal display is used. The display contains a special chemical called liquid crystal. When electric current is applied to parts of it, those parts turn black to make the figures. This technique is also used in computer graphics and pocket TVs.

▷ The hands and figures on this watch face are coated with a special chemical which is "luminous" — it glows in the dark. The light is produced by the chemical and lasts for a long time.

COLORED LIGHT AND COLOR

Theater sets use artificial colored light to change the colors on stage. You can try this yourself. Draw the colors of the spectrum on a piece of white cardboard. Cover a flashlight with red cellophane so it produces red light. In a dark room look at the cardboard with the red light. Some of the colors will appear shades of red (those which reflect red light) and some will appear black. Try the same experiment with blue cellophane.

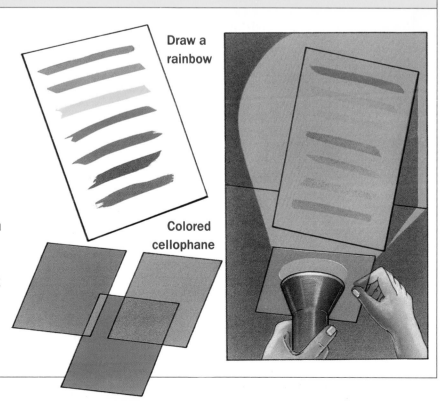

Draw a rainbow

Colored cellophane

Green plants need carbon dioxide, water and sunlight to make new substances. To use the chemicals they get from the plants they eat, animals need oxygen from the air, and they give out carbon dioxide. Plants and animals depend on each other to keep the balance of different gases in the air.

PHOTOSYNTHESIS

Plants take in carbon dioxide from the air and water from the soil, and make chemicals such as cellulose, starch and sugar from them. The plants then use these chemicals to make stems, leaves and roots. To do all this a plant needs energy in the form of sunlight and a special substance called chlorophyll, which is found in the leaves. This process is called photosynthesis.

△ The sunflowers in the photograph all face the same direction. Plants always grow toward the light since they need light in order to make the chemicals with which they make stems, leaves and roots. Without light, plants grow thin and spindly and eventually die.

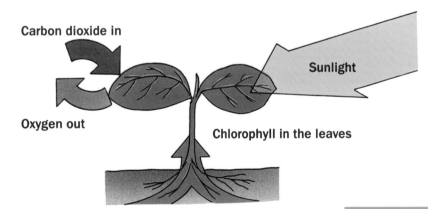

Carbon dioxide in

Sunlight

Oxygen out

Chlorophyll in the leaves

Water and minerals are taken through the roots

MORE ABOUT LIGHT AND PLANTS

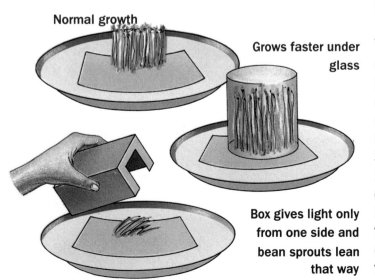

Normal growth

Grows faster under glass

Box gives light only from one side and bean sprouts lean that way

You can find out more about plants by doing these investigations with bean sprouts. Bean sprouts grow quickly and easily so you will get results in a few days. Take three saucers and place some damp blotting paper in each one. Sprinkle some bean seeds on top of each blotting paper. Place an upturned glass over one set of seeds and a box with a hole cut in one side over another. Leave the third set to grow normally. What differences do you expect to see between the sets of seeds when they grow?

CAMOUFLAGE

Many animals have different colors and patterns on their skins or coats which make them difficult to see. They are "camouflaged." Camouflage helps to protect an animal from predators. Polar bears, for example, have white coats which camouflage them in snow. Camouflage may also help the predator. Tigers' stripes help them to hide in long grass when they are hunting prey. Some animals have bright colors that warn off other animals. Some butterflies have patterns like eyes on their wings. These frighten away birds which might otherwise eat them. Other animals use color to attract a mate. The male stickleback fish has bright blue eyes and a red chest which helps him attract a female in the mating season.

▽ Can you see the lizard? Its mottled brown skin merges well with the stone background. The lizard is difficult to see until it moves.

△ This glow-worm can produce its own light which it flashes to attract a mate. Different types of glow-worms produce different patterns of light.

Light is a type of radiation. But the light we see is only a small part of the radiation which comes from the Sun. A lot of the Sun's radiation is in the form of infrared and ultraviolet rays, two types of radiation which we cannot see. They are part of the "invisible spectrum."

THE INVISIBLE SPECTRUM

Although we cannot see infrared or ultraviolet rays we can feel their effects. Ultraviolet light causes skin color to darken and can be harmful. We feel infrared as heat. There are also other types of radiation which we cannot see.

All this radiation travels at the same speed – the speed of light, which is about 300 million meters per second (over one thousand million kilometers per hour). The radiation travels as "waves" rather like ripples in a pond. The only difference between the different types of radiation is the lengths of their waves (wavelengths) and their effects.

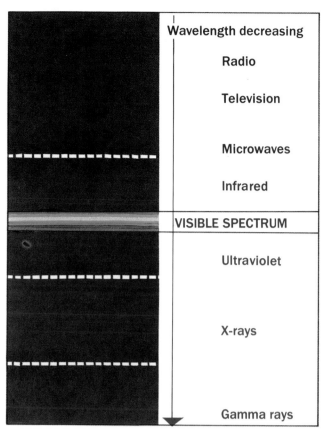

Wavelength decreasing

Radio

Television

Microwaves

Infrared

VISIBLE SPECTRUM

Ultraviolet

X-rays

Gamma rays

△ The diagram shows the main types of radiation. They all have different wavelengths. Radio waves have the longest and gamma rays have the shortest.

PROTECTION FROM INFRARED RADIATION

Set up two glasses of water as shown in the diagram. Put them both out in the sun. Take the temperature of the water in each glass every half hour for about two hours. Which one heats up more quickly and which one gets hotter? Then put the glasses in a cool place out of the sun. Which one cools down faster? What effect does metal foil have on infrared radiation?

Which one is warmer?
Which one heats up faster?

Metal foil

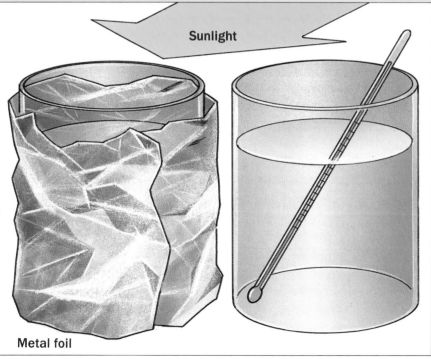

Sunlight

ENERGY FROM THE SUN

It is possible to collect and use energy from the Sun to provide heat and hot water for homes. To do this solar panels are used. These panels are usually installed in the roof and are arranged to face the Sun for as much of the day as possible. Some can even be turned during the day to follow the path of the Sun. Solar panels are black so that they absorb the Sun's radiation. Below the surface there is a fluid, usually water, that heats up when the panels get hot. The hot water can then be used for washing or can be fed into radiators to heat rooms. In places with sunny climates, solar panels can be used to provide most of the energy needed for the home. In colder parts of the world, solar panels can be used together with other sources of energy such as electricity. The advantage of using the energy of the Sun is that it is free and, unlike fossil fuels, will not run out.

△ Solar panels provide energy for homes without damaging the environment or wasting limited resources.

▽ You cannot see or feel ultraviolet light but you may see and feel its effects if you sunbathe for too long.

ULTRAVIOLET RADIATION

The color of your skin depends on the amount of a pigment called melanin it contains. Melanin helps to protect your skin from the harmful effects of ultraviolet light. In sunshine your skin will produce more melanin to protect you. But if your skin is fair and you lie in sunshine it is likely to burn. A lot of exposure to ultraviolet light may also cause skin cancer. It is best not to lie in hot sunshine but if you do you should use suntan lotion which will give your skin extra protection. The diagram shows how the lotion works. When it is spread over the surface of the skin it forms a protective barrier. It reflects some of the ultraviolet light away before it reaches you. Different strengths of lotion reflect different amounts of ultraviolet and protect you to different extents.

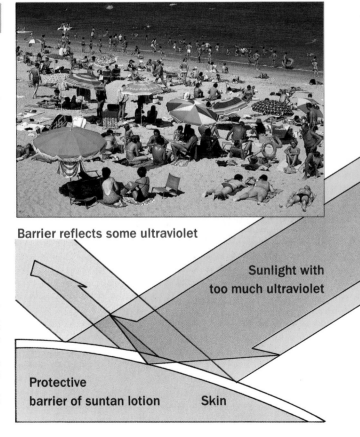

Barrier reflects some ultraviolet

Sunlight with too much ultraviolet

Protective barrier of suntan lotion

Skin

Lasers are machines which produce a special kind of light. Laser light can be focused onto a very small spot and cause intense heat. Lasers can "cut" (burn) through steel! Laser light has many uses — in industry, in surgery, to make holograms and compact disks and for taking accurate measurements.

WHAT MAKES A LASER?

Ordinary light is made up of many colors. But laser light contains light of just one wavelength. Whereas in ordinary light the waves travel in different directions, in a laser the light waves travel in the same direction and in step with each other. The diagram shows how a laser works. Inside the laser is a tube filled with a chemical. Energy is supplied to this chemical which makes it produce light. Some of this light bounces backward and forward between the two mirrors. But some shines through the hole and emerges as a beam of laser light.

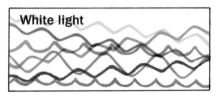

Many wavelengths out of step

Single wavelengths in step

△ Sometimes laser light is used for entertainment. This spectacular laser show is produced by beams of laser light. Laser light can travel long distances without fading.

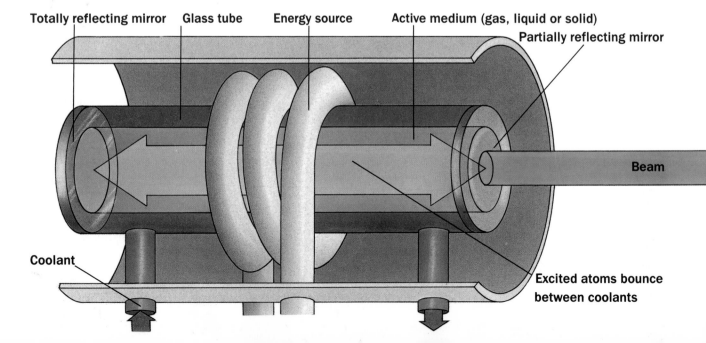

Totally reflecting mirror · Glass tube · Energy source · Active medium (gas, liquid or solid) · Partially reflecting mirror · Beam · Coolant · Excited atoms bounce between coolants

LASER SURGERY

Precision lasers are used by surgeons. Laser beams make excellent "knives." They are sterile and seal up small blood vessels as they cut, reducing bleeding. Their most common use is in eye surgery. If the retina becomes separated from the back of the eye, a laser beam can weld it back into place without the need to cut open the eye. Lasers are also used to remove stomach ulcers. The laser is directed into the body through a tube which the patient swallows. Outside the body lasers are used to treat skin growths and remove tatoos. Dentists may also use lasers instead of a drill to remove decay from teeth.

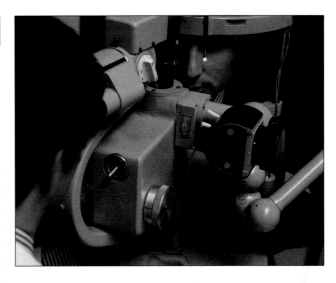

△ A laser can be directed into the eye in order to repair the retina.

▽ A hologram can appear as a 3-D image and can be very realistic.

HOLOGRAMS

A hologram is a type of photograph which is made with a laser. Unlike ordinary photographs holograms are three dimensional. They look solid and real and even appear different from different angles — just like a real object. The reason holograms look so real is that they are accurate recordings of the light reflected from an object. Many uses are being found for holograms. They are very difficult to forge and so are being used on credit cards.

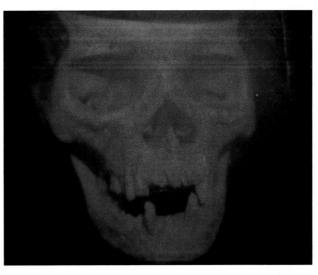

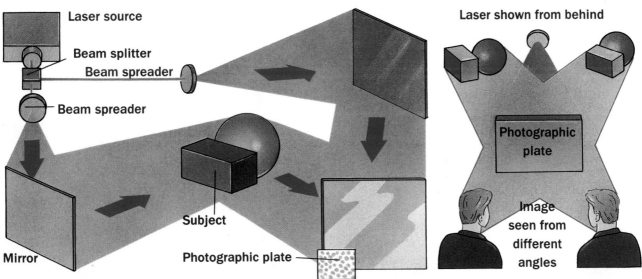

Laser source
Beam splitter
Beam spreader
Beam spreader
Mirror
Subject
Photographic plate

Laser shown from behind
Photographic plate
Image seen from different angles

Over the years people have found out more and more about how light behaves and how it is used. Some of the important discoveries and inventions are on this page — from Isaac Newton's discovery of the spectrum to the latest in videodisks which use the most advanced laser technology.

Galileo

Newton

The laser

Laser technology is quite a recent but important invention. The first laser was not built until 1960. It was built by T.H. Maiman in the United States. It contained a specially made ruby rod and produced pulses of red laser light. Later in the same year a gas laser was invented in the U.S. This laser produced a continuous laser beam. The invention of lasers has had a great effect on modern technology. One example is the recent invention of the compact disk. The C.D. is a high quality, long lasting alternative to the record or cassette. The recording consists of tiny pits in the disk which are "read" by a laser beam. The disk is only 5 inches across but can play for an hour. Compact disks were first produced in 1982. Videodisks have also been invented. These work in a similar way to C.D.s, but the information they carry is converted into a picture on a television screen.

Galileo and telescopes

When Galileo was alive (1564-1642) most people believed that the Earth was the center of the universe and that the Sun moved around it. Galileo spent a lot of time studying the sky with telescopes which he built himself. He discovered that in fact the Earth, with the other planets, traveled around the Sun. He also discovered that the Moon has a mountainous surface and that Jupiter has its own moons. Galileo used refracting telescopes. But in 1668 Isaac Newton invented the first reflecting telescope using mirrors. Newton made many contributions to our understanding of the universe. He discovered that white light could be separated into the colors of the spectrum with a glass prism.

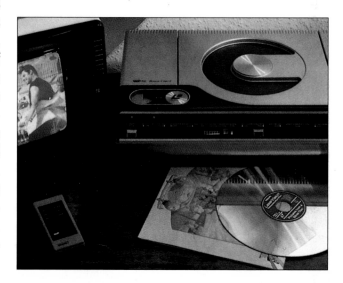

Chromatography
A way of separating different colored substances in a liquid.

Color blind
A condition where a person cannot tell the difference between two or more colors, for example red and green. It is more common in boys than in girls.

Focus
Adjust to make a clear image.

Image
The picture of an object which is produced by a lens or a mirror.

Magnify
Make an image appear bigger.

Optic nerve
A long string-like structure which carries messages from the eye to the brain.

Periscope
A device with two mirrors to help you see around corners.

Primary color
A color which cannot be made by mixing other colors. The primary colors of light are red, green and blue. The primary colors of pigments are yellow, cyan and magenta. All other colors can be made by mixing the primary colors.

Radiation
The carrying of energy by waves. These waves are part of the electromagnetic spectrum.

Reflection
When light bounces off a surface we say it is reflected. Everything reflects some light.

Refraction
When light passes from one substance to another it usually changes direction. We say it is refracted. Refraction takes place because light travels faster through some materials than others.

Signal
Information carried as waves which is received by the television.

Transmitter
Apparatus which sends out signals.

Wave
A way in which energy travels from one place to another.

Wavelengths
Each different type of radiation has a different wavelength. Radio waves have the largest wavelength and gamma rays have the shortest. Each different color of visible light has a different wavelength. In fact, color is really wavelength and all of the different colors travel with different speeds through different substances. Red light travels fastest, violet light is the slowest. In a vacuum all colors travel at the same speed.

Photographic credits:
Cover and pages 7, 13, 19, 25 (top), 28 and 29 (bottom): Science Photo Library; page 5: Rex Features; pages 6 and 9: Robert Harding Library; pages 8 both, 10, 13 (top), 15, 17, 25 (bottom) and 27 (bottom): Zefa; pages 11, 12, 18 and 22 both: Chapel Studios; page 21: Spectrum; pages 23 and 29 (top): Paul Brierley; page 24: Photosource; page 27(top): SERI; page 30 (top and middle): Popperfoto.